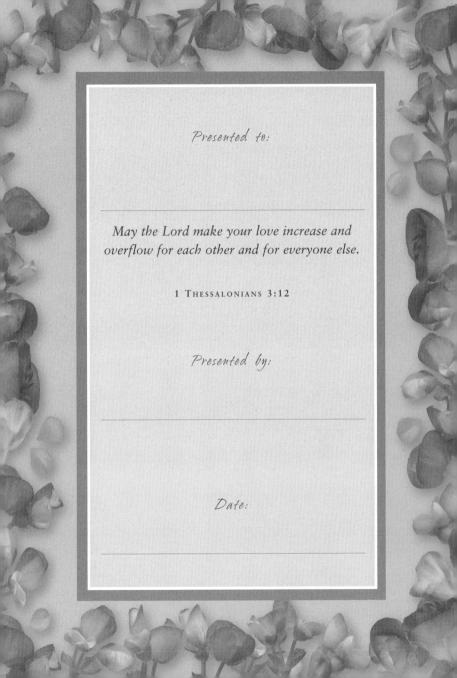

Presented to:

_____

May the Lord make your love increase and
overflow for each other and for everyone else.

1 THESSALONIANS 3:12

Presented by:

_____

Date:

_____

Celebrate Love

*Heartwarming Stories,
Inspirational Sayings, and
Loving Expressions
for Couples*

WHITE STONE BOOKS
LAKELAND, FLORIDA

Celebrate Love:
Heartwarming Stories, Inspirational Sayings,
and Loving Expressions for Couples

ISBN 1-59379-059-7

Copyright © 2006 by Bordon Books, Tulsa, OK
Published by White Stone Books
P.O. Box 2835
Lakeland, Florida 33806

Printed in Mexico

Manuscript written and prepared by SnapdragonGroup℠ Editorial Services

Contents

*Love is an irresistible desire to be
irresistibly desired.*

R OBERT F ROST

Introduction

Romantic love—it's elusive, enchanting, incredibly debated, and at times, poorly defined. Everyone desires to be loved, but few, if any, fully understand it. Love can take us to the heights and to the depths of emotion. It can bring out our best and worst. We seek it because, even in the darkest hour, love makes us feel alive. And when it's brightened and enhanced by the light of God's love—it becomes powerful and life-changing.

Celebrate Love was created with the illumination of God's love in mind. Romantic love—once offered to Him—is a thing of beauty: selfless, pure, hopeful, patient, humble, faithful, and caring—and that's just for starters. You will see beauty in these pages, but it is our prayer that you will see even more beyond the lines of poetry and the uplifting stories. We hope you will be able to walk away with a deeper understanding of the romantic love in your life and practical ways to live and love to the fullest.

*There are three things that
will endure—faith, hope,
and love—and the gretaest
of these is love.*

1 Corinthians 13:13 NLT

Love Is Patient
and Kind

Love suffers long and is kind;

love ... does not behave rudely,

does not seek its own,

is not provoked.

1 CORINTHIANS 13:4–5 NKJV

Fulfillment

There is no happier life
But in a wife;
The comforts are so sweet
When two do meet.
'Tis plenty, peace, a calm
Like dropping balm;
Love's weather is so fair,
Like perfumed air.
Each word such pleasure brings
Like soft-touched strings;
Love's passion moves the heart
On either part;
Such harmony together,
So pleased in either.
No discords; concords still;
Sealed with one will.
By love, God made man one,

Yet not alone.
Like stamps of king and queen
It may be seen:
Two figures on one coin,
So do they join,
Only they not embrace.
We, face to face.

WILLIAM CAVENDISH
English Poet
1592-1676

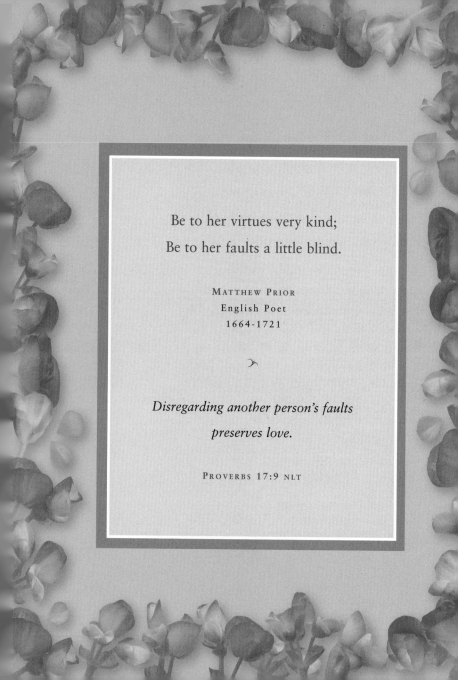

Be to her virtues very kind;

Be to her faults a little blind.

MATTHEW PRIOR
English Poet
1664-1721

Disregarding another person's faults

preserves love.

PROVERBS 17:9 NLT

Patience and Kindness

- Let your love supersede the pressures of the moment. Later, during a peaceful time, discuss options to use in working out your differences.

- Be supportive and eager if you are called upon to help with a task your sweetheart has started, but don't take over and try to do it yourself.

- Applaud a job well done.

- Voice your appreciation for even the most mundane tasks.

- Pick up the phone and call your beloved when you are running late.

- Verbalize a genuine compliment.

- Put a note from a "secret admirer" where your loved one will find it.

- When you've been apart, greet each other with a kiss.

- Speak as kindly and courteously to your beloved as you would a friend or business acquaintance.

- Listen carefully and don't interrupt.

- Overlook weaknesses and focus on strengths and virtues.

13

*H*eavenly Father,

Knowing You want us to have a relationship
that is beautiful and characterized by the fruit of
patience and kindness, show us ways in which we
can bless one another with kind words and loving
actions. Give us creative ways to add spice and
enjoyment to our marriage, those things that will
make it a pleasure to be together.

During those times when anger would be the
easiest reaction, help us respond with a kind tone
of voice and a pleasant expression on our faces.
Allow that kindness to draw us together. Help us
remember that we're on the same team!

In those moments when we are frustrated and
under stress, help us to be patient with one
another—the way You are patient with us. Teach us
to treat one another with the same courtesy we
easily extend to our friends—so that we might
create a deep, meaningful, lifelong friendship with
our loved one.

AMEN.

Spread love everywhere you go: First of all in your own house ... let no one ever come to you without leaving better and happier.

MOTHER TERESA
Nobel-Peace-Prize Recipient
1910-1997

Clothe yourselves with tenderhearted mercy,
kindness, humility, gentleness, and patience.
You must make allowance for each other's faults and
forgive the person who offends you. ...The most
important piece of clothing you must wear is love.
Love is what binds us all together
in perfect harmony.

COLOSSIANS 3:12–14 NLT

Real Romance

Inever dreamed that faith in my husband's romance quotient would be restored the night the septic tank exploded. I was in the combination utility room/downstairs bathroom completing my nightly routine of throwing in one last load of laundry before heading upstairs to bed when I heard it—an odd rumbling sound growing in intensity and volume. It sounded like a scary combination of growling dragons and starved lions.

With difficulty I turned my eight-month pregnant body from the washer-dryer platform toward the source of the noise—the toilet—and gingerly lifted the lid. Without further ado, a part of life that I generally spend time avoiding literally hit the fan.

I bolted from the room, shouting my husband's name. "Greg! Ohhhhhh, Greg. Oh, no. I REALLY need you!" He skidded around the corner, obviously anticipating a premature trip to the hospital. He looked somewhat relieved when he saw me—until I pointed out the brown geyser spurting from the toilet toward the ceiling and quickly flooding the floor.

Greg sent me to call for help, while he dashed outside to remove the lid from the clean-out valve, releasing the pressure from the erupting septic tank. After I located a 24-hour septic service and heard their assurance that they would be out early the next morning, I plopped my sizable bulk into a chair and waited for Greg to come back inside.

"Go on to bed," he urged. "I don't want you around all these chemicals and there really isn't any way you can help," he said, pushing me toward the stairs and then bending over to kiss the tip of my nose.

I trudged upstairs, dressed for bed, and then pressed my nose against the glass panes of our bedroom window. In the moonlight I saw my husband make trip after trip, mop and buckets in hand, out to the farthest acre, dumping his "fertilizer," and returning again and again. This was one quirk of this crazy old farmhouse we'd been restoring that I couldn't deal with—especially now.

In the morning I tiptoed downstairs quietly. I walked through each room, the acrid smell of fresh bleach assailing my nostrils. I wrinkled my nose, but curiosity got the best of me. My eyes widened as I took in the sight—there was not a sign of water, silt, or that other stuff anywhere! The bathroom gleamed. A brand-new mop and bucket stood guard by the sink and new bathmats and a toilet cover graced the floor and throne, courtesy of my husband and the local supercenter.

Greg quickly appeared with a smile on his face. After giving me a huge hug—from the side of course—he whispered in my ear, "Did I do all right, honey? Everything seem okay to you?" My gratitude was palpable! Forget the diamonds; fancy vacations—nothing but trinkets compared to a husband who is willing to tackle an exploding septic tank!

Moments later, ready to leave for school, I backed down the long gravel drive, carefully looking in the rearview mirror. Reflected there I saw further evidence of true love. In blue glass chalk, my husband had drawn a gigantic heart on the back window of the minivan. In backward letters so they would read correctly in the mirror were the letters GD + CD = True Love Forever. "Yes," I said prayerfully. "I am a blessed woman."[1] 💜

Defining Romance

Perhaps, like me, you need to rethink your definition of romance. Growing up, my sister and I were always hounding our daddy. "Be romantic! Get Mom some flowers; take her to dinner; buy her surprises." He usually ignored us. But after his death from cancer at the young age of fifty-six, we noticed something was missing from Mom's life—real romance. You see, for thirty-four years my mother had never filled her car with gasoline, washed, or vacuumed it. She had never once driven to work or back home on snowy roads; Daddy had always done it for her. He gave of himself for her benefit, and I feel sure she found that a better definition of romance than all the flowers or dinners in the world.

Being Patient and Kind

For Him

Today, I will purpose to be mindful of how precious and valuable my loved one is to me and reflect that by being patient and kind, I am showing my gratitude to God for placing the gift of her presence in my life. I will support her in her goals and dreams and be there when she needs me. I will love and encourage her and make every effort to treat her with the same patience and kindness that Jesus has shown toward me.

For Her

Today, I will honor God by showing patience and kindness toward my loved one and remember that he is a gift from God. I will express genuine appreciation for the things he does for me—both big and small—abandoning a demanding, nagging attitude and replacing it with gratitude. I pledge to trust in the work God is performing in his life by speaking words of encouragement and offering him my support and love.

Be the living expression of God's kindness;
kindness in your face, kindness in your eyes,
kindness in your smile,
kindness in your warm greeting.

MOTHER TERESA
Nobel-Peace-Prize Recipient
1910-1997

Be kind and compassionate to one another,
forgiving each other,
just as in Christ God forgave you.

EPHESIANS 4:32

Love Is Humble
and Caring

Love cares more for others than for self.

1 CORINTHIANS 13:4 THE MESSAGE

Friendship

Oh, the comfort—the inexpressible comfort

of feeling safe with a person,

Having neither to weigh thoughts,

Nor measure words—but pouring them

All right out—just as they are—

Chaff and grain together—

Certain that a faithful hand will

Take and sift them—

Keep what is worth keeping—

And with the breath of kindness

Blow the rest away.[2]

DINAH MARIA MULOCK CRAIK
Poet and Novelist
1826-1887

Marriage has in it less of beauty, but more of safety,

than the single life; it has more care, but less danger;

it is more merry, and more sad; it is fuller of sorrows,

and fuller of joys; it lies under more burdens, but it is

supported by all the strengths of love, and charity,

and those burdens are delightful.

JEREMY TAYLOR
British Preacher and Theologian
1613-1667

Two are better than one,
because they have a good return for their work:
If one falls down,
his friend can help him up.
But pity the man who falls
and has no one to help him up!

ECCLESIASTES 4:9-10

Humility and Caring

➤ Resist the urge to say, "I told you so."

➤ Let your sweetheart have the last word.

➤ Face the world together—don't compete against each other.

➤ Each should take a genuine interest in the other's activities.

➤ Each should be available to listen when the other person needs to talk. Don't offer advice unless it is asked for.

➤ Be respectful and affirming when your sweetheart is upset about something—even if it seems minor to you.

➤ Be the first to say, "I'm sorry."

➤ Admit when you are wrong.

➤ Make a point to hold hands and be generous with your hugs.

Special Moments

If a scientific study were done to prove that "opposites attract," my husband and I would make the perfect test couple. I've lost count of all the times people have said, "You two are just soooo different."

Truer words were never spoken. He's organized; I'm not. He's a loner; I'm a people person. He thinks I'm too laid back while other family members and I often playfully refer to him as "Mr. Intense." There's a sign above our kitchen stove depicting a big bear wearing an apron that reads, "Real Men Wear Aprons, Buddy." He *is* a real man in every sense. He often cooks more than I do. And he does wear an apron at times. The sign that most describes me, however, is of a female bear wearing glasses that reads, "Organized People Are Just Too Lazy to Get Up and Look for It."

When it comes to special occasions, Harvey leans toward practical gift giving. I, on the other hand (at least in Harvey's opinion), tend to be impractical and a little wild and wacky, going to extremes to make a memory. Whenever I disagree on this issue, he always reminds me of the year I almost rented a real chimpanzee for his birthday.

I was determined to make it a birthday Harvey would never forget. He loves to go to the zoo and is especially intrigued with the monkeys in their cages. He's always jokingly said how much fun it would be to have a monkey— if you didn't have to deal with all the monkey maintenance.

One day as I was reading the local paper, I spotted an ad for a chimp. Sam and his owner, Stan, entertained for birthday parties.

Perfect, I thought. Harvey's birthday is only a week away. I picked up the phone and dialed Stan's number.

But it was not to be. Two hundred dollars for fifteen minutes, and we had to provide a meal for Stan and the chimp!

When Harvey's birthday arrived, I prepared him an extra special steak dinner without the monkey business and gave him a funny card that said, "I have good news and bad news." Inside it said, "The good news is that I've rented forty dancing girls for your birthday. The bad news is that they're all about your age!" Then I told him about almost getting him a dinner date with the chimp of his dreams, but that it was way beyond our already stretched budget. I saw the true meaning of the saying "it's the thought that counts" when just hearing about the idea brought a huge smile to his face.

Over the years, Harvey's become a little more comfortable with my way-out antics, and we've learned to embrace our differences while keeping an understanding of one thing: It's not only okay to create special moments in our marriage, it's essential. We have our challenges like anyone else, but the little things that have given our relationship its own personality and strength have been instrumental in overcoming any crisis we've ever had to face.

Soon after we met, Harvey and I gave each other nicknames: "Daddy Bear" and "Baby Bear." Strangely enough, these nicknames have become a common bond that overrides our very different personalities. They've been instrumental in keeping our hearts young toward each other.

I'll never forget our first Christmas when, on Christmas morning, Harvey awoke to find a giant stuffed teddy bear with his name on it under the tree. He looked like a little boy as he smiled, hugged his bear, and said, "I can't believe you got me—a grown man—a teddy bear, but I love it." From that moment, bears became a standard gift for birthdays, Valentine's Day, and anniversaries. Harvey even puts together an "Easter Bear" basket for me every year. While I'm asleep, he places it by the bed for me to find when I wake up. Little does he know that the "moment" I enjoy most is seeing the twinkle in this big brawny bear's eyes, just knowing he's made such an effort to do something special for me.

Although Harvey fills a doorway with his presence and sometimes comes across as serious and straightforward, I know the truth. Underneath is a teddy bear with a compassionate heart as big as the sky. Tears come easily when he sees someone who's hurting. My favorite snapshot of Harvey was taken last spring. In his big, strong hands, he's holding a tiny blue jay he rescued after it fell from its nest. Moments like these I frame and place upon the wall of my heart.[3] ♥

Love Is Pure
and Holy

Keep yourself pure.

1 TIMOTHY 5:22

January 10, 1846

Dear Elizabeth:

Do you know, when you have told me to think of you, I have been feeling ashamed of thinking of you so much, of thinking of only you—which is too much, perhaps. Shall I tell you? It seems to me, to myself, that no man was ever before to any woman what you are to me— the fulness must be in proportion, you know, to the vacancy ... and only I know what was behind—the long wilderness without the blossoming rose ... and the capacity for happiness, like a black gaping hole, before this silver flooding. Is it wonderful that I should stand as in a dream, and disbelieve—not you— but my own fate?

Was ever any one taken suddenly from a lampless dungeon and placed upon the pinnacle of a mountain, without the head turning round and the heart turning faint, as mine do? And you love

me more, you say?—Shall I thank you or God?
Both,—indeed—and there is no possible return
from me to either of you! I thank you as the
unworthy may and as we all thank God. How
shall I ever prove what my heart is to you? How
will you ever see it as I feel it? I ask myself in
vain. Have so much faith in me, my only
beloved, as to use me simply for your own
advantage and happiness, and to your own ends
without a thought of any others—that is all I
could ask you without any disquiet as to the
granting of it.

May God bless you!

Your B.A.[4]

LETTER FROM ROBERT BROWNING

(English Poet 1812-1889)

to Elizabeth Barrett Browning

(English Poet 1806-1861).

Theirs is one of the world's most famous romances.

H eavenly Father,

You are such a good God! You've taught us to value ourselves as Your holy and unique creations, worthy of honor. It is our deepest desire to protect that insight by being faithful and true in our relations with each other, in regard to our physical bodies, as well as to our thoughts and loyalties. May we always do what is pleasing to You.

Help us, Lord, to remember that showing respect for each other in this way is not something we will find much support for in the world. We will look to You instead, to keep us rightly aligned with Your pure and holy intentions for our relationship. We ask that You would watch over us and give us a quick nudge if You see we are headed for a misstep. In this way, we believe we will receive the greatest happiness in our lives together.

A MEN.

There is nothing holier in this life of ours than the first consciousness of love—the first fluttering of its silken wings—the first rising sound and breath of that wind which is so soon to sweep through the soul, to purify or to destroy.

HENRY WADSWORTH LONGFELLOW

Beloved American Poet

1807-1882

December 30, 1915

My Love:

Off you go again alone and it's with a very heavy heart I part from you. No more kisses and tender caresses for ever so long—I want to bury myself in you, hold you tight in my arms, make you feel the intense love of mine.

You are my very life, Sweetheart, and every separation gives such endless heartache. Goodbye my Angel, Husband of my heart. I envy my flowers that will accompany you. I press you tightly to my breast, kiss every sweet place with tender love.

God bless and protect you, guard you from all harm, guide you safely and firmly into the new year. May it bring glory and sure peace, and the reward for all this war has cost you.

I gently press my lips to yours and try to forget everything, gazing into your lovely eyes—I lay on your precious breast, rested my tired head upon it still. This morning I tried to gain calm and strength for the separation. Goodbye wee one, Lovebird, Sunshine, Huzy mine, Own![5]

Your Alexandra

LETTER FROM TSARINA ALEXANDRA FYODOROVNA
(1872-1918) to Tsar Nicholas II of Russia (1868-1918)

Love Song

There is a strong wall about me to protect me:
It is built of the words you have said to me.

There are swords about me to keep me safe:
They are the kisses of your lips.

Before me goes a shield to guard me from harm:
It is the shadow of your arms between me and danger.

All the wishes of my mind know your name,
And the white desires of my heart
They are acquainted with you.
The cry of my body for completeness,
That is a cry to you.
My blood beats out your name to me, unceasing, pitiless
Your name, your name.

MARY CAROLYN DAVIES
American Poet
c. 1914-1934

They Call It Puppy Love

Several years ago our then college-age daughter decided she really wanted a dog to keep her company, so she bought a blonde, cocker spaniel puppy. A week later she called and changed her mind.

"I love this puppy, but she is keeping me up yelping all night! I have to get up all hours of the night and take her outside. (She lived in an upstairs apartment). I thought it would work, but I think we need to sell her. Would y'all take her and try to sell her for me?"

I grinned, thinking of all the "wee hour" feedings my own daughter had brought into my life years before. We reluctantly agreed, and placed an ad in the paper the following week. Two weeks passed, and a single woman finally answered our ad and agreed to pick up the dog the next morning. But by this time, I knew it was puppy love at first sight. Even though the dog had chewed on woodwork, shoes, and toes, my heart was already attached to that precious puppy. When I watched her being carried out of our lives the next day, I couldn't hold back the tears. As we watched the dog and her new owner leave, Larry reached over and gave me a tender reassuring hug—nothing unusual.

I grieved over my lost love but knew life must return to normal. I was unprepared for the phone call the next morning, however. The young lady who bought the dog was pleading on the other end of the line. "My landlord won't let me keep her in our apartment complex," she said. "He says she will grow up to be too big. I have to get rid of her. Would you consider giving me my money back and taking the dog back?" What else could we do?

So the young lady brought the puppy back the next day. But as she was turning to leave our home, she said to me, "You know, someday I want a marriage like yours."

I was clueless. I hadn't told her anything about my marriage. She knew absolutely nothing about us except that we had sold her a puppy. "What do you mean?"

"You know, the way your husband hugged you when I left the other day," she explained. "I could tell you love each other by the look in your eyes."

It was a simple observation, but we got the message. Romance is not just for us to enjoy as husband and wife. People are actually watching us to see if the flame is alive. Only a few years earlier, we had experienced some fresh, romantic emotions and a renewed relationship after some rocky times in our marriage. Each of us had become much more intentional about special caring behaviors such as hand-holding, hugs, planned dates together, and even surprises. But we were amazed that a simple thing like a special look or reassuring hug could be a model of successful love to an observer. It offers hope for those whose relationships are still lacking.

We've now been married thirty-nine years, and we are still holding hands, planning dates, and trying to out-surprise the other. Someone once said, "Love seeks not limits but outlets." We took our cue from the One who loves unconditionally—the Lord Jesus Christ—who has unlimited outlets in showing His love for us. Although we fall short of His kind of love, His is a perfect model for us.

In case you are wondering what happened to the young lady, God opened the door that day she brought the puppy back for us to introduce her to God's great love. A woman with great emotional needs, she unloaded her burden and started a "sacred romance" with God that day that we pray is still flourishing.

Oh, and that sweet cocker spaniel puppy? We already had two dogs, but there's always room for love. Especially puppy love. "Brandy" is gone now, but for eleven years, she brightened our home. And we've never forgotten the lesson she taught us about the power of romance—and hope and love.[6]

She Walks in Beauty

She walks in beauty, like the night
Of cloudless climes and starry skies;
And all that's best of dark and bright
Meet in her aspect and her eyes:
Thus mellow'd to that tender light
Which heaven to gaudy day denies.

One shade more, one ray less,
Had half impair'd the nameless grace
Which waves in every raven tress,
Or softly lightens o'er her face;
Where thoughts serenely sweet express
How pure, how dear their dwelling place.

And on that cheek, and o'er that brow
So soft, so calm, yet eloquent,
The smiles that win, the tints that glow,
But tell of days in goodness spent,
A mind at peace with all below,
A heart whose love is innocent!

LORD BYRON

Most Colorful of the English Romantic Poets

1788-1824

*Love does not consist in
gazing at each other,
but in looking outward together
in the same direction.*

ANTOINE DE SAINT-EXUPÉRY
French Aviator and Author
of Extraordinary Children's Literature
1900-1944

Love Is Filled with Hope

Hope does not disappoint us, because God has poured out his love into our hearts by the Holy Spirit, whom he has given us.

ROMANS 5:5

Sweet Peril

Alas, how easily things go wrong!
A sigh too much, or a kiss too long,
And there follows a mist and a weeping rain,
And life is never the same again.

Alas, how hardly things go right!
'Tis hard to watch in a summer night,
For the sigh will come, and the kiss will stay,
And the summer night is a wintry day.

And yet how easily things go right,
If the sigh and a kiss of a summer's night
Come deep from the soul in the stronger ray
That is born in the light of the winter's day.

And things can never go badly wrong
If the heart be true and the love be strong,
For the mist, if it comes, and the weeping rain
Will be changed by the love into sunshine again.[7]

GEORGE MACDONALD
Scottish Novelist, Poet, Clergyman, and Children's Book Author
1824-1905

*H*eavenly Father,

   Life is wrought with challenges. If it weren't for
You, we would surely be without hope. But we aren't
without You! In fact, You are the God of hope and
You promise to answer when we call!

   You know the problem that is confronting us, and
we ask You to intervene. With man, this situation is
impossible, but with You, all things are possible. This
gives us hope.

   When the storms of life threaten, our tendency is
to pull away, to blame, to take out our frustration on
one another. But this isn't Your way. Give us the
grace to pull together in love, to draw so close
together that nothing can separate us. Instead of
speaking words that hurt or tear down, we want to
speak only words of love and encouragement.

   In You, there is always hope. We can rest, trusting
that You will work out everything for our best.
AMEN.

Hopefulness

❧ Practice looking on the bright side. There's always a silver lining for those who will seek it.

❧ Christians are never without hope. Find Bible promises regarding an area in which your loved one is struggling. Share the verses and use them as the basis for prayer.

❧ Don't let the problem turn you against each other. Face it together, head-on. The two of you, together with God, are a majority.

❧ Pray together, taking one another by the hand.

❧ Offer support without criticism.

❧ Make suggestions sparingly, and always say them in a positive manner, couched in much love.

❧ Take your concerns about each other to God in prayer. He can produce lasting change where it is needed.

❧ Meditate on God's Word instead of the circumstances.

A Prodigal Romance

My husband, Mike, and I were married in a pagan wedding on Wind 'N Sea Beach in LaJolla, California, on June 27, 1976—barefoot. Both sets of parents mumbled their disapproval in the predawn light and shivered in the cold wind blowing off the Pacific.

Oblivious, Mike and I faced the morning star and pledged our undying love, while offering up sacrificial bowls of fire and water, symbols of our spiritual union. Blissfully happy, we ignored our parents grumbling and sealed our vows in accordance with the state of California.

For years my mother kept asking, "Are you sure you're legally married?" I'm the first one to admit that the chances of our "hippie" marriage lasting were about nil, but God knew what He was doing when He brought us together.

I met Mike the first day I moved from Chicago to the San Francisco Bay area. Because of failed first marriages and other relationships that had left us heartbroken, we had both sworn off dating for life. But the night before we met at our place of employment, Mike had a dream about me and was told I would be his wife. Nutty! But it was the seventies, and we were both into mysticism and alternative religions. From the moment we met, we were in love.

Thirteen days later, Mike invited me out for lunch at a seafood restaurant at Fisherman's Wharf in San Francisco, and later we drove to Golden Gate Park, where he found the perfect tree on the perfect hill with the perfect light to propose. I said yes the next day. We hid our relationship from our parents until just before the ceremony.

For the seven years after our pagan rite of marriage, we continued to search for God until He tapped us on the shoulder and said He was right there. Life had been a struggle, with battles over stepchildren and betrayals by supposed friends.

One October afternoon, Mike and I were weary of life and staring at one another across the table. All at once, we both said at the same time, "Why don't we find a church?" It startled both of us. We had never talked about Christianity and certainly never considered going to church. Mike had been raised an Episcopalian. Since my parents didn't attend services, I often went to whatever church my friends attended, whether it was Baptist, Methodist, or Catholic.

The sermon that Sunday morning was about the Prodigal Son returning home. We were prodigals who had slopped spiritual hogs until our Heavenly Father cleaned us up and welcomed us with open arms. After a lengthy process, I was baptized and confirmed, and just to make sure our marriage was blessed by God, we were "remarried" on our seventh anniversary. Christ was now at the center of our marriage, holding us together.

As we grew in faith, we grew in love for one

another. Mike's an incurable romantic and for years brought home a single rose for me every payday. I left lipstick love notes on the mirror for him, and we still hold hands in public, laughing at each other's corny jokes.

Mike's mother once said we were like two old comfortable shoes, walking side by side through life. She was right. I can't imagine what life would have been like without him. Would I have found someone like Mike who still kisses me every morning and says, "I love you"? Or would I have continued to slide into an ill-spent life and ended up bitter and alone?

Like most married couples in their late fifties, we've seen the best and worst of life. We've endured the deaths of our parents, two heart surgeries for Mike, and a pulmonary embolism for me. We've celebrated the marriages of Mike's children, and a granddaughter is now part of the family. We've faced life head-on with passion—together.

It's been almost twenty-nine years since we said our vows to one another on that sandy California beach. While other people saw our quirks and flaws, God saw our hearts and knew He could shape and mold us into vessels fit to serve Him.[8] 💜

January 23, 1935

My darling Clemmie,

In your letter from Madras you wrote some words very dear to me, about my having enriched your life. I cannot tell you what pleasure this gave me, because I always feel so overwhelmingly in your debt, if there can be accounts in love. ...What it has been to me to live all these years in your heart and companionship no phrases can convey.

Time passes swiftly, but is it not joyous to see how great and growing is the treasure we have gathered together, amid the storms and stresses of so many eventful and to millions tragic and terrible years?[9]

Your loving husband,

Winston

LETTER FROM WINSTON CHURCHILL
(One of the greatest statesmen in world history
1874-1965) to his wife, Clemmie.
They were married fifty-six years.

$\mathcal{T}$he day after Jack Benny died, a single, long-stemmed red rose was delivered to Mary Livingstone Benny, his wife of nearly 48 years. After several days, with another rose delivered each day, Mary called the florist to find out who was sending them. The florist told her that Benny had made arrangements for a rose to be sent to her every day for the rest of her life and had included a provision in his will for the deliveries—a touching and romantic final gesture for a man born on Valentine's Day.

Inspiring Hope

For Him

My Heavenly Father says that He is the God of hope, and because He lives in me, I am empowered to be a beacon of hope to my beloved when she is discouraged or disheartened. More than anything, I want to be sensitive to what she is going through and take it upon myself to find encouraging scriptures to bolster her faith. Nothing is impossible with our God, and I take pleasure in reminding her of this often. As we pray together, we will present her concerns to Him, trusting Him for the outcome.

For Her

My beloved shoulders a lot of responsibility; therefore, I will be faithful to pray for him. I will make an extra effort to be sensitive to what he is going through and endeavor to support him with my words and my actions. I will make it my task to find ways to lighten his load and his day with hope and joy that comes from the Lord. I will endeavor to make my words daily reminders that the God of the universe is working on his behalf and He will faithfully fulfill His promises. With Him, we always have hope.

Love Is Faithful and True

Love ... takes pleasure in
the flowering of truth.

1 CORINTHIANS 13:4, 6 THE MESSAGE

Believe Me, If All Those Endearing Young Charms

Believe me, if all those endearing young charms,
Which I gaze on so fondly to-day,
Were to change by to-morrow, and fleet in my arms,
Like fairy-gifts fading away,
Thou wouldst still be adored, as this moment thou art,
Let thy loveliness fade as it will,
And around the dear ruin each wish of my heart
Would entwine itself verdantly still.

It is not while beauty and youth are thine own,
And thy cheeks unprofaned by a tear,
That fervor and faith of a soul may be known,
To which time will but make thee more dear!

THOMAS MOORE
Irish poet who wrote the words for
some of the best-loved songs in the English language.
1779-1852

Knit your hearts with an unslipping knot.

WILLIAM SHAKESPEARE

Greatest Dramatist Ever Known, Finest English-Language Poet,

and World's Most Popular Author

1564-1616

I am my beloved's, and my

beloved is mine.

SONG OF SOLOMON 6:3 KJV

57

December 23, 1782

My Dearest Friend,

Should I draw you the picture of my heart it would be what I hope you would still love though it contained nothing new. The early possession you obtained there, and the absolute power you have obtained over it, leaves not the smallest space unoccupied.

I look back to the early days of our acquaintance and friendship as to the days of love and innocence, and, with an indescribable pleasure, I have seen near a score of years roll over our heads with an affection heightened and improved by time, nor have the dreary years of absence in the smallest degree effaced from my mind the image of the dear untitled man to whom I gave my heart.
Abigail

LETTER FROM ABIGAIL ADAMS
(1744-1818) to her husband, John Adams
(Second president of the United States 1735-1826)

Faithfulness and Truth

🕊 Determine to be your loved one's best friend, one who is loyal to the end.

🕊 Renew your marriage vows on your anniversary. Remind yourself of those reasons you first fell in love.

🕊 Talk about growing old together. Develop a long-term vision of the future with each other in it. Put it on paper.

🕊 Stand up for your sweetheart. Only speak well of him or her.

🕊 Work out problems together. Avoid the temptation to go to other family members regarding conflict between the two of you.

🕊 Pray for each other daily.

🕊 Do everything in your power to help the one you love with problems he or she might encounter.

🕊 Always speak the truth, but do it with love and tenderness.

🕊 Always have your sweetheart's best interest in mind.

🕊 When you confide in each other, don't tell another living soul.

Being Faithful and True

For Him

My sweetheart owns my heart. I want to be her knight in shining armor, especially in the area of my character. In the world, the line between right and wrong has become so blurry, but I will strive to do what is right, according to God's Word. Many people will come and go from her life, but I want to be someone she can count on to be there when she needs me. I choose to be true to my word and faithful to her in every way. I will be the best friend she could ever have, faithful and true to the end.

For Her

I want to be faithful and true, someone my sweetheart can count on. I won't treat the truth lightly but will make sure that I follow through on my promises. "Little white lies" have no place in me, nor does any form of deception. I will be utterly truthful in all of my dealings so that the one I love knows what he can expect of me. I hope that I will never give him any reason to doubt me.

H eavenly Father,

Faithful and true—what a perfect description of You! No matter what, because of Your great love, You are always faithful and true to us. You always stick by us. You never let us down.

Lord, we want these things to be said of us! The union between my sweetheart and me is holy, and we want to always be loyal and true to You and to each other. May we be faithful to pray for one another, to stand up for each other, to be loyal in thought, word, and deed.

When the wind and the rain of life's circumstances beat against us, when others let us down, enable us to find solace in the fact that no matter what, we will be there for one another—just like You are there for us, ever faithful and true.

AMEN.

When Opposites Attack

I was only thirteen when an incredible six-foot, fifteen-year-old guy sat down beside me in church. I knew it was a sign from heaven that he was the one. So what if the seat next to me was the only one available?

Larry and I survived a long teen romance and then headed for college. After my freshman year, we were married on a "wing and a prayer" and rode off on a white horse named Blissful Ignorance.

In spite of our clueless beginnings, we managed to live for quite some time in what most would call a fairy-tale marriage. The formula was easy. If Larry asked me what I wanted to do, I gave the safe answer, "I don't know, Honey. Whatever you want to do."

Gradually, I discovered we had some major differences. He sorted; I tossed. He cleaned; I swiped. He filed; I piled. He folded; I stuffed. The hall closet served as our disorganized battleground.

For a long time, I thought Larry had a photographic memory. I, on the other hand, was always forgetting something. Then he told me his secret: He made lists. Lists? What's a list?

One evening, I was trying to remember an important phone number when Larry asked me his favorite question: "Why didn't you write it down, Rebecca?"

"I did, Honey. On a very important envelope flap."

Larry raised his eyebrows.

"Oh, no, Larry—you didn't! It was right here on the kitchen cabinet, next to some notes I'd scribbled on that paper napkin."

"Sorry, Hon," he replied matter-of-factly, "but I think the garbage men just took off with your catsup-stained files."

Traveling together proved quite a challenge for Larry also, but eventually he grew accustomed to my pre-takeoff whine of apology made halfway to the airport. "Honey, I think I forgot something."

"What did you forget this time?"

"Hairspray, toothpaste, mouthwash—" He'd roll his eyes with that "not-again" look.

"Rebecca," he said once, "we're going to be late. Didn't you make a list?" He quickly pulled a U-turn, and we sped back home to retrieve my missing items. As usual, we hopped on the plane just as they were closing the gate.

Don't get me wrong. We often laughed about our differences. But there were a few times when nothing seemed funny anymore. Fortunately, Larry and I both had parents who made it through tough times together. That knowledge, coupled with God's constant faithfulness, helped bolster our confidence that we could work out our problems.

By the time we discovered our emotional distance,

we knew that giving up was not an option. We also knew that counseling was in order. So with fresh battle scars and a determination to nestle, instead of wrestle, and a lot of help from God, we embarked on a journey to find our lost love.

We looked again at our lofty dreams and earnest promises—"for better or worse, for richer or poorer" (lots of "poorer"). We relived both the floods and the refreshing showers, and on the horizon we caught a dim vision of what our marriage could become.

Getting there was another matter! First I had to discard my dog-eared script of "Sleeping Beauty Meets Prince Charming"—and with much prayer, we wrote the first chapter of our new life together.

As we grow older, most married couples look back wistfully on the early years of struggle and wish we could have known then what we know now. But life doesn't work that way. God, in His wisdom, knows that struggle—like the butterfly emerging from its cocoon— is an important part of growth and freedom. The places where we get stuck are the instruments God uses to infuse us with Christ-like character. And in marriage, opposites—like magnetic poles—attract each other to the very strengths God knows we need.

Months later we were basking in our newfound relationship when Larry leaned over and gave me not a peck, but a long, lingering kiss and embrace.

As if awakened from a deep sleep, I dreamily responded with the words I knew my own Prince

Charming longed to hear. "Say! How about we light some candles, turn on some romantic music, and clean out the hall closet tomorrow?"

With a twinkle in his eye, Larry replied gallantly, "Better write it down."[11]

There is nothing so loyal as love.

ALICE CARY
American Poet
1820-1871

Love Is Always Believing

Love ... always looks for the best.

1 CORINTHIANS 13:4-7 THE MESSAGE

Heavenly Father,

Help us to always believe the best in one another. Rather than focusing on our weaknesses, let us search for the treasure that You see in us. When You look at us, You see not just what we are at that moment, but You also see what we can become in the future with Your help. Give us the eyes of faith to see as You do.

When we met, we were both looking for someone who would be there through thick and thin. When one of us is discouraged, experiencing guilt or pain, use the other to speak an encouraging word. Give us a word in season to refresh and lift one another up.

Love always believes the best. Help us to always do the same

AMEN.

I believe in the sun even when it is not shining;
I believe in love even when I do not feel it;
I believe in God even when He is silent.

AUTHOR UNKNOWN

O Lord! Look at me ...
through eyes of mercy and forgiveness,
through eyes of everlasting love and kindness.

PSALM 25:6-7 TLB

Always Believing

For Him

Sometimes my beloved is insecure. She struggles with her appearance, wonders if she's doing all that she can to be a good person, wonders if she's covering all of the bases on her job. I want to help her see what a jewel she is to me and to others. I will make it a point to tell her every day that I believe in her and appreciate all that she does for me. I will point out her strengths and remind her of the attributes I fell in love with in the first place. When she forgets the compliments that others have paid her, I'll remind her of them. I want to be her biggest fan—patting her on the back for her accomplishments, both big and small—and let her know how proud I am of her.

For Her

I want to be a personal cheerleader for the man I love, the one he can always count on for support and an encouraging word. Neither one of us is perfect, but I choose to focus on his positive traits, the strong points that I fell in love with. I will dwell on these and put all negative thoughts out of my mind, striving to do the things that bring out the best in him. I trust God to complete the good work He has begun in this good man, and I'll always believe in him.

Believing in Each Other

➢ Always believe the best of each other.

➢ Ask God to help you see each other the way He does.

➢ Minimize your loved one's weaknesses and limitations and focus on the best and strongest attributes.

➢ Often verbalize your faith in the one you love: "I believe in you! You can do it!"

➢ Tell your beloved that you are available to help and support when needed—and mean it.

➢ Take concerns about each other to God. Ask Him to help your sweetheart reach his or her full potential.

➢ Choose to believe God's Word. Negative circumstances can't change the truth of God's promises, but God's Word can change any circumstance.

Love, Honor, and Trust

Married just over twenty-four hours, my bridegroom and I began the first full day of our honeymoon in a sun-drenched, snow-covered, Rocky Mountain lodge.

It was a morning filled with both expectation and exasperation. Expectation because, on the downhill side of midlife, I'd discovered love. Exasperation, because I'd married the leader of a National Ski Patrol team. My sweetheart from Montana had skied for thirty years. I, on the other hand, couldn't tell one ski from another.

The agreement before we married was that I'd never have to ski. But it was obvious that five months out of every year I wouldn't see much of him while he was on ski patrol.

"It won't be that bad," my bachelor had said. "But, Babe, it's up to you."

It took several weeks of wrestling, but once I decided, there was no turning back.

"I'm skiing," I said, "and I don't care to discuss it again."

Now, however, as I opened the drapes and faced the mountain, I despaired. We'd agreed I'd stay on the bunny hill in the beginners' class—with the children!

When I slammed drawers and refused breakfast, my

husband just wrapped his arms around me and said, "Babe, you'll do great." How could I resist such charm?

Outside our room, where wind-whipped snow bit into my face, I squeezed into enormous boots and measured the incline and distance to the Ski School Chalet.

"I can't do it!" I said.

"Yes, you can," Scotty said, grinning. "I'll get you down that hill. It's easy. Just trust me."

I squinted toward the lodge's main room, where warm smoke curled above Arizona stone. This man had been skiing forever, while I'd spent years indoors. Trust him? I don't think so!

But as if he'd read my thoughts, Scotty hugged me and chuckled, emphasizing how short the distance would seem.

"Oh, all right," I said. "I'll do it."

The plan was to join forces—literally. Scotty explained I'd stand behind him and slip my skis between his. He'd ski...I'd coast. I'd also press my face into his jacket, wrap my arms around his middle, and close my eyes.

"Close my eyes?" I shrieked.

Again he smiled in reassurance. Then volunteering one final optimistic pledge, he patted my gloved hands, shouted "Yahoo!" and pushed off.

"This is kind of fun," I mumbled against my partner's broad back.

"What'd I tell you?"

Scotty threw his head back. I knew he was laughing, but I couldn't hear him for the crackling ice and snow sprays echoing across the hill. He patted my hands, said something about "not to worry" and "just hang on." And, to my surprise and his, I did exactly as instructed. However, near the bottom of the grade, we picked up speed.

Scotty had explained we'd accelerate "a bit." But hearing him tell it and experiencing this sensation were two different things. I'd been given his promise that we wouldn't fall, but my skis were spreading apart, and my faith was fading fast.

"How much farther?" I barely managed.

"We're doing great," my husband said. "Just relax."

Scotty's words meant absolutely nothing. My fears and my evaluation of our chances had become all the proof I needed that we would crash. I froze.

"Relax!" Scotty shouted back over his shoulder.

"I can't!"

"You've got to, Babe! We're nearly there! Trust me!"

Although he tried to prevent it, within seconds I had tipped over and thrown my spouse off balance as well. Suddenly, four skis, three poles, one pair of goggles, and two prime-of-life bodies were rolling, slipping, and bouncing across an unrelenting, ice-covered knoll. Not three feet from our target, all my hopes had come to a painful end.

As quickly as a bruised man can, Scotty brushed

snow from his glasses, questioned me about broken bones, and gathered up his gloves.

"Babe," he said, "do you know what you did?"

I could only splutter. My pride had suffered and I was certain I'd had all I could bear, until I heard one of my husband's buddies. "Hey! This must be the new bride!"

"She learning to ski?" another whooped.

"She sure is," Scotty laughed. He pressed his lips to my wounded ear. "And learning to trust too. Right, Babe?"

"Right," I barely managed, feeling my husband's reassuring arms around me and praying he was right—praying this had been one of God's little lessons and that, before long, I really would learn how to trust him.[12]

A happy marriage is the union of two good forgivers.

ROBERT QUILLEN
American Journalist
1887-1948

Love Is Ever Forgiving

Love ... doesn't keep score
of the sins of others.

1 CORINTHIANS 13:4-5 THE MESSAGE

Heavenly Father,

Surely when Jesus told us that we might have to forgive up to seventy-seven times, He knew relationships would often require it. I marvel at Your ability to forgive and forget, no matter what we've done. Help us to do likewise. You know it doesn't come naturally. It's much easier to get mad, shift blame, put down, or retaliate; but that is not Your way.

Although forgiving someone doesn't mean allowing yourself to be abused, it does mean letting the offender go and entrusting that person to You. Holding on to anger and bitterness only hurts the one bearing the grudge. Its destructive power eats away like cancer and will destroy the one who holds it.

We want to love the way You do. Help us not to keep a running tab on each other's transgressions, but to let go quickly. Give us the grace to wipe the slate clean and begin anew.

AMEN.

Love is an act of endless forgiveness, a tender look which becomes a habit.

PETER USTINOV
English Actor and Versatile Man of Letters
1921-2004

If you are angry, don't sin by nursing your grudge.
Don't let the sun go down with you still angry—
get over it quickly; for when you are angry
you give a mighty foothold to the devil.

EPHESIANS 4:26-27 TLB

Ever Forgiving

For Him

I won't allow a wall of bitterness to be erected between my beloved and me. I won't put a guilt trip on her or condemn her when she hurts me. Instead, I choose to forgive her and do what I can to resolve the conflicts between us. Even if she doesn't apologize, I will forgive her anyway and ask God to forgive her as well. Our relationship is too valuable to allow anything to come between us. As I do my part to initiate forgiveness, my trust will be in God that He will minister to her heart and give her the grace to work things out with me.

For Her

I will not pout or hold a grudge when my beloved says or does something that hurts me. Instead, I'll be open with him about my feelings. Then I will ask God to help me let it go. With His help, I know I can forgive and even forget. When I am at fault, I will be quick to apologize to the one I love so much and ask God to forgive me as well. Most of all, I will be diligent to protect the bond of love in our relationship from the resentment and anger that results from unforgiveness.

Forgiving Each Other

- Make every effort to resolve conflict. Don't sweep problems under the rug.

- Take responsibility for your part in the conflict.

- Ask God to heal you of any hurt or brokenheartedness. Receive His love and acceptance.

- Don't try to get even.

- Don't nurse a grudge.

- Don't withhold your love.

- Be quick to forgive.

- Make a decision to forgive, even if your feelings are telling you otherwise.

- Verbalize your forgiveness.

- Don't try to change the one you love. Ask God to help you change anything in you that needs to be corrected. Entrust your sweetheart to God.

- Once you forgive an offense, don't bring up the issue again or use it against your sweetheart.

Coming Clean

My husband, Scotty, had been traveling three weeks out of every four. We had prayed for a job change—a move to a place where the pace would be slower and our time would belong to us—but God's answer seemed to be no.

To add to my frustration, the weather was cold and rainy—fifteen degrees below the springtime norm—and crabgrass had taken over our yard. So had dandelions, grubs, and moles.

Now after too much rain and too much time alone, I wanted my husband to comfort me—to talk to me. Scotty, on the other hand, had been arbitrating meetings for weeks. All he wanted was to be left alone.

I don't remember the last straw after he got home, but I do remember bounding down our cellar stairs, jaws clenched, and seizing a comforter—one I'd stuffed into a bag months before because it didn't fit into my washing machine and would have to be taken to the Laundromat. It would be my excuse to run away from home. If my husband wouldn't listen to me, I'd retreat to eating candy bars and reading magazines at the Laundromat.

With the comforter spinning, I seated myself on a plastic chair. I tried to concentrate, but I couldn't stop thinking about my "inconsiderate spouse." The man hadn't listened to one single word I'd said! Yes, I understood these separations made life difficult for him, too. But he didn't have to be so insensitive.

"Men! They're all alike!" I murmured.

That's when I spotted a woman who'd once waited on me at a discount store. Looking weary and old before her time, she was loading not one washer but eight—odd for someone who seemed to have nothing to wear.

While I watched, she trudged to the coin machine, bought soap, returned to reserve a string of washers, jammed coins into the machines, dumped in detergent, slammed lids, slapped plastic baskets down on the concrete floor, and lit a cigarette.

She worked all day, every day. Now she would spend her free time doing eight loads of laundry? At our house, we seldom had more than two. Much of what my husband wore, he took to the cleaners so I wouldn't "have to deal with it."

I pictured Scotty with his arms full of jackets and slacks, grinning and asking if I wanted to ride along, proposing breakfast out or coffee on the way home.

But, this morning, he'd made me so mad.

I'd no sooner set my face like flint, when the other woman's husband appeared, shoulders slouching, bill cap on tilt, denims dangling from nearly invisible hips, a brown cigarette in one corner of his mouth, and wearing a frown. He hadn't said one word to his wife, when two teenaged girls bounded through double doors to join the pair.

Oh, good, I thought, *they're all going to help.* But

they weren't. The girls wanted money for a Coke machine, and the man wanted multiple kisses planted on his skinny mouth. Giggling, the daughters departed, while the man leaned against a washer to coach his wife. Maybe he was just waiting until he'd finished his smoke. Then he'd give her a hand. Scotty would!

Instead, the man lit another cigarette, while his wife literally ran from washers to dryers and back.

"Help her!" I wanted to shout.

"You gonna be done pretty soon?" the sullen man asked, as if he had plans and his wife was holding him back.

She nodded, drew smoke deep into the shell of her lungs, and dragged her frame on shabby shoes across the floor for more quarters.

For the next half hour, the woman worked and the man tapped his lips with his forefinger when he wanted another smooch—while his daughters exited and returned at predictable intervals to announce they needed more cash and wished their mother would "Hurry up."

I don't believe this! I thought. If I had all that wash, Scotty would never expect me to manage alone!

The nights he was home, didn't he dry dishes for me? And what about mornings? While I cooked breakfast and packed his lunch, didn't he make the bed? When he needed a shirt, didn't he usually iron it himself? Had he once complained? The other husband's abrasive voice interrupted my dawning truth.

"Maybe I'll go see what the kids are up to," he said.

Go see what the kids are up to? Help your wife! I stood straight up out of my chair. "Scotty would," I mumbled aloud, stepping toward the dryer.

My husband suddenly walked through the door and seemed to fill the room. He was still wearing the faded shoes he'd donned to dig in his garden because, "Gardens can't wait!" He wore the goofy shirt he'd "captured" from my giveaway bag, because he planned to root poison ivy out of my flower bed. "Won't disappear by itself," he'd said.

"Scotty! Why are you here?" I blurted, thinking how even when he was agitated his blue eyes gave away his tenderness.

"Babe…" His voice was husky. "I haven't been very good to you." Clearing his throat, he stuffed his hands into denim pockets, like the cowboy he'd been when we met.

Feeling like the heroine in a western romance, I wanted to fling my arms around his neck and tell him he was forgiven.

"You're much more important than any garden," he said, squeezing my hand. "Besides, it gets lonely at home when you're not there."

I wouldn't cry and I wouldn't kiss my husband in a laundromat. But I was tempted.

"Your comforter done?" Scotty asked.

I'd forgotten I owned a comforter. I nodded. "I just

have to fold it and then—"

He turned his back. He wasn't listening? He was leaving?

"Come on, Babe," he said, smiling over his shoulder. "I'll give you a hand." At the dryer door, he unwound the tulips and leaves and reached across the fabric to squeeze my hand. "I'm taking you to lunch."

I glanced at the woman whose wash was nearly dry. She'd be folding clothes forever. I glowered at her spouse who was mumbling something about "going for ice cream with the girls."

No longer caring what strangers thought, I touched the laugh lines on Scotty's face and kissed his cheek. I told him I was sorry, I loved him, and I was grateful for the marriage we shared. I admitted I'd been having more than a little trouble with the frequent separations.

"Me, too, Babe," Scotty said, his palm warm and comforting at the back of my neck.

Our folding finished, I turned sideways to catch one last glimpse of the slouching man squinting at his watch and tapping his boot at his overworked wife.

"I'm glad you're my husband," I whispered, tucking my fingers into Scotty's strong hand as we headed for the door. "Even if you do travel."[13] ♥

As we grow in wisdom,
we pardon more freely.

Anne-Louise-Germaine de Staël
French Author
1766-1817

May the Master of Peace himself
give you the gift of getting along with each other
at all times, in all ways.

2 Thessalonians 3:16 The Message

Love Is Selfless and Serving

Love ... isn't always "me first."

1 CORINTHIANS 13:4.5 THE MESSAGE

*H*eavenly Father,

Jesus said that He did not come to be served but to serve. Help us to cultivate this attitude in our relationship, resisting the urge to demand our own way. If we give way to that urge, it will surely take its toll on our relationship. Help us to choose the high road instead, choosing to serve one another in love.

Father, thank You that we don't have to rely solely on our human love. You knew we would need the kind of love that You have, and You've filled our hearts with it. Teach us how to yield to it so that it will freely flow between us. Bring to mind ways in which we can be a blessing to each other and put each other first. Help us to lay down our lives in love every single day—just as Jesus did.

AMEN.

In submission we are free to value other people. Their dreams and plans become important to us. We have entered into a new, wonderful, glorious freedom, the freedom to give up our own rights for the good of others. For the first time we can love people unconditionally. We have given up the right for them to return our love. No longer do we feel that we have to be treated in a certain way. We can rejoice with their successes. We feel genuine sorrow at their failures. It is of little consequence that our plans are frustrated if their plans succeed. We discover that it is far better to serve our neighbor than to have our own way.

MOTHER TERESA
Nobel-Peace-Prize Recipient
1910-1997

Do not use your freedom to indulge the sinful nature; rather, serve one another in love.

GALATIANS 5:13

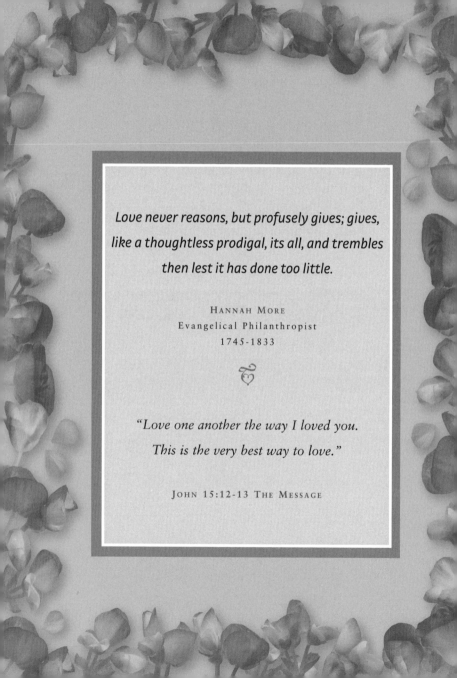

Love never reasons, but profusely gives; gives,
like a thoughtless prodigal, its all, and trembles
then lest it has done too little.

HANNAH MORE
Evangelical Philanthropist
1745-1833

"Love one another the way I loved you.
This is the very best way to love."

JOHN 15:12-13 THE MESSAGE

Selflessness and Service

- Fix your loved one's favorite meal or go to his or her favorite restaurant.

- Do the little things like cleaning up after dinner.

- Ask if there's anything you can bring your sweetheart if you leave the room.

- Provide something refreshing to drink when the one you love is working hard on a project.

- Take your delightful darling on a date to do his or her favorite pastime.

- Quit what you are doing and make eye contact when you are speaking to each other.

- Offer to do your sweetheart's least favorite chore.

- Fill up the gas tank on your beloved's car.

Love and the Big "C"

"Puppy Love," "I'm All Shook Up," and "Love Me Tender" are titles and lyrics that bombard us over the golden-oldie airwaves. The entertainment industry embellishes love, cheapens love, and idealizes love. But in the reality of the Christian life, love is serious, deeply moving, and a personal expression of service and selflessness.

I married the love of my life nineteen years ago, and the Lord blessed us richly. We own a home, have two beautiful daughters who are godly teens, and have a strong family bond. Our household is filled with giggling teenagers, pizzas in the freezer, and lots of hugs, kisses, and kidding around. My husband and I are both teachers who love our jobs and are dedicated to helping others grow in their education.

But in a matter of a few short weeks, our secure world imploded when I was diagnosed with the big "C" word—cancer. All our hopes and dreams for the future seemed now in doubt.

Experiencing some vague feelings of fullness and soreness in my abdomen, I made an appointment with my family physician. A CT scan revealed two very large and suspicious ovarian cysts. Surgery was scheduled to remove the cysts, but we wouldn't know the full diagnosis until later.

Following the operation, I was groggy from the anesthesia but resting comfortably. After a day of prayer and waiting, my husband finally said a teary goodnight. In my heart I was fearful that the news would be bad. And it was. The surgery and biopsy confirmed our worst nightmare—ovarian cancer.

After release from the hospital, I convalesced at home and met with an oncologist to discuss my treatment options and the plan of attack. Chemotherapy began just three weeks after surgery. So much had changed, yet the love of God, family, friends, and especially my husband remained ever strong and upheld me as I walked through my dark valleys.

Since my diagnosis, recovery from surgery, and now during my treatments, my husband and daughters have taken over the usual, mundane household chores I usually did. Grocery shopping has become a fun outing for them. They come home with all sorts of "fun foods" that I usually try to limit.

Love doesn't always have to be expressed with a bouquet of roses or a romantic candlelight dinner or a gift of diamonds. We experience love in the day-to-day tasks of life. In the midst of grocery shopping, doing laundry, and washing dishes, my husband and children have shown their love and selfless support for me. They've helped me to see that the material things of this life are temporary and insignificant compared to the great love we have for each other and our Lord.[14] ♥

He who loves another
tries truly to understand
the other.

HARRY A. OVERSTREET
Social Psychologist, Educator, Lecturer
1875-1970

Love Is Wise and Understanding

The wisdom that comes from heaven is first of all pure;
then peace-loving, considerate, submissive, full of mercy and
good fruit, impartial and sincere.

JAMES 3:17

*H*eavenly Father,

When we fell in love, we were drawn to the strengths we saw in each other. Where one of us was weak, the other was strong. And that's the way You planned it—so we would complete each other.

But now that we've moved deeper into our relationship, those differences grate on our nerves at times. They can divide us if we let them. We need Your wisdom and insight to know how we can work together as a team. Instead of fighting, we ask You to show us how we can combine our strengths and achieve what we couldn't have alone.

Help us to put ourselves in the other's shoes. Give us understanding so we will be able to see beyond the actions to the intent. Teach us how to celebrate our own uniqueness as a couple and truly become one.

Amen.

Wisdom and Understanding

➣ Be eager to listen, slow to speak.

➣ Don't try to discuss a problem when you are feeling emotionally charged.

➣ Don't point out your loved one's shortcomings; take them to God in prayer if they are bothersome.

➣ Look to the Bible for answers to your problems.

➣ Each of you should put yourself in the other's shoes and try to see things from their perspective.

➣ Don't jump to conclusions or make mountains out of molehills.

➣ Resist the urge to judge.

➣ Never nag.

➣ Don't let problems reach a critical point before trying to resolve them. Nip them in the bud.

➣ Seek counseling when needed.

A Wife Gives Thanks

Critically, I watched my husband as he stood inside the main entrance in his red usher's jacket, greeting people, passing out bulletins, welcoming newcomers to our church. *How I wish he wouldn't wear that old tie,* I thought. *And why did he cut his hair that short?*

My judgmental thoughts were interrupted by our pastor calling the ushers to the altar. Four went forward—one did not. The one was my husband. He was fumbling under a seat for the offering basket he'd set down while talking to a new family.

"For heaven's sake," I murmured, watching as my spouse hastily retrieved the basket, stretched his long legs, and caught up with the others.

Lately everything he did got on my nerves. How many times I wished he were different. If only he enjoyed traveling. Why couldn't he learn to swim? Why hadn't he been promoted, so we could get that transfer back home?

Honestly! Why doesn't he get with it? my thoughts murmured. Immediately, I heard God speak to my spirit.

Read Job 14:3, God said.

Lord! How about if I look it up at home? Our pastor is speaking and getting ready to lead us in prayer.

But, the thought returned. *Read Job 14:3 now!*

Anxious to get back to the pastor's teaching, I grabbed my Bible and flipped pages, located the scripture passage, put my finger under the verse, and read, *"Must you be so harsh with frail men, and demand an accounting from them?"* (TLB).

Harsh with frail men? Tears filled my eyes as God's words pierced my heart. I first glanced up toward the altar at our pastor and then turned my head to watch my husband ambling back up the aisle with those long, slow strides of his. My heart pounded, but my harping thoughts had silenced. In the midst of the service, God had gotten my attention with private instruction meant only for me.

As my spouse slipped into the pew and squeezed my hand, my heart cried out, *Father, forgive my silent sins against my husband! He didn't hear me, but You did. Thank You for helping me see what I was doing. Thank You for this man beside me. Thank You for the love this man shows when, with his lunch pail, he sets out for work each day, even before the sun has risen. Thank You for the care he gives the dog I hauled home from the pound. Thank You for the hours he spends at the kitchen table, helping our daughter with her math or paying bills for orthodontists and dresses for the prom.*

Thank You for the times he's cared for me when I was so desperately ill. Thank You for the bird feeder he built for me outside our kitchen window. Thank You for all the hours he's spent with me at flea markets, loaded down with all the "good deals" I couldn't resist, and for the times he's escorted me to plays—just because I love the theater—and baseball games, and thanks for our shared hot dogs at the park.

Thank You for picnics beside a mountain stream and hikes in the moonlight to glimpse a herd of elk grazing in summer grass.

Thank You, Lord, for this unique man—quiet, patient, dependable. Most of all, thank You for letting me see in him a small reflection of the unconditional, protective love You have for us.

I turned to look at my husband again and smiled.

"Amen," I said softly. "Amen."[15] ♥

What Is Love?

AN ESSAY BY HELEN KELLER
Born Blind and Deaf, She Became a Beloved Advocate
for the Disabled
1880-1968

I remember the morning that I first asked the meaning of the word "love ..." Miss Sullivan put her arm gently round me and spelled into my hand, "I love Helen."

"What is love?" I asked. ...

"Love is something like the clouds that were in the sky before the sun came out," she replied. ... "You cannot touch the clouds, you know; but you feel the rain and know how glad the flowers and the thirsty earth are to have it after a hot day. You cannot touch love either; but you feel the sweetness that it pours into everything. Without love you would not be happy or want to play." The beautiful truth burst upon my mind—I felt that these were invisible lines stretched between my spirit and the spirit of others.

Love Is
Never Ending

Love ... never looks back,

but keeps going to the end.

1 CORINTHIANS 13:4, 7 THE MESSAGE

The Newly Wedded

Now the rite is duly done,

Now the word is spoken,

And the spell has made us one

Which may ne'er be broken;

Rest we, dearest, in our home,

Roam we o'er the heather:

We shall rest, and we shall roam

Shall we not? together.

From this hour the summer rose

Sweeter breathes to charm us;

From this hour the winter snows

Lighter fall to harm us:

Fair or foul—on land or sea—

Come the wind or weather,

Best and worst, whate'er they be,

We shall share together.

Death, who friend from friend can part,

Brother rend from brother,

Shall but link us, heart and heart,

Closer to each other:

We will call his anger play,

Deem his dart a feather,

When we meet him on our way

Hand in hand together.[16]

WINTHROP MACKWORTH PRAED
English Poet and Essayist
1802-1839

They that love beyond the world cannot be separated by it. Death cannot kill what never dies, nor can spirits ever be divided that love and live in the same divine principle.

WILLIAM PENN
English Quaker Who Founded Pennsylvania
1644-1718

"Haven't you read," [Jesus] replied, "that at the beginning the Creator 'made them male and female,' and said, 'For this reason a man will leave his father and mother and be united to his wife, and the two will become one flesh'? So they are no longer two, but one. Therefore what God has joined together, let man not separate."

MATTHEW 19:4–6

O woman! lovely woman! Nature made thee
To temper man: we had been brutes without you.
Angels are painted fair, to look like you:
There's in you all that we believe of heaven,—
Amazing brightness, purity, and truth,
Eternal joy, and everlasting love.

THOMAS OTWAY
English Dramatist
1652-1685

"This is it!" Adam exclaimed.
"She is part of my own bone and flesh! Her name is 'woman'
because she was taken out of a man." This explains
why a man leaves his father and mother and is joined to his
wife in such a way that the two become one person.

GENESIS 2:23–24 TLB

July 14, 1861

My very dear Sarah:

The indications are very strong that we shall move in a few days—perhaps tomorrow. Lest I should not be able to write you again, I feel impelled to write lines that may fall under your eye when I shall be no more. ...Not my will, but thine O God, be done. If it is necessary that I should fall on the battlefield for my country, I am ready. I have no misgivings about, or lack of confidence in, the cause in which I am engaged, and my courage does not halt or falter.

But, my dear wife, when I know that with my own joys I lay down nearly all of yours, and replace them in this life with cares and sorrows ... is it weak or dishonorable, while the banner of my purpose floats calmly and proudly in the breeze, that my unbounded love for you, my darling wife and children, should struggle in fierce, though useless, contest with my love of country?

The memories of the blissful moments I have spent with you come creeping over me, and I feel most gratified to God and to you that I have enjoyed them so long. And hard it is for me to give them up and burn to ashes the hopes of future years, when God willing, we might still have lived and loved together and seen our sons grow up to honorable manhood around us. ...My dear Sarah, never forget how much I love you, and when my last breath escapes me on the battlefield, it will whisper your name. ...O Sarah, I wait for you there! Come to me, and lead thither my children.

Sullivan[17]

LETTER FROM UNION SOLDIER SULLIVAN BALLOU

(1829-1861)

to his wife, Sarah, while awaiting orders that would take him to Manassas, where he and twenty-seven of his men would die one week later at the Battle of Bull Run.

Young love is a flame; very pretty, often very hot and fierce, but still only light and flickering. The love of the older and disciplined heart is as coals, deep—burning, unquenchable.

HENRY WARD BEECHER
Eloquent, Dramatic, and Witty Protestant Preacher
1813-1887

Many waters cannot quench love,
neither can the floods drown it.

SONG OF SOLOMON 8:7 KJV

Never Ending

> Talk about what it will be like to spend eternity together.

> Discuss the issue of divorce. Once you've agreed that it should never be an issue now or in the future, drop the word from your vocabulary.

> Ask God to bring unity to "irreconcilable differences." He has a wonderful plan for your lives together. Hook up with it, regardless of your feelings.

> A loving relationship shouldn't be a drudgery or bondage. Ask God to help you make it heaven on earth.

> Remind each other of the special times you've shared. Rejoice about the victories you've achieved together. Remind each other of the hopes and dreams you shared early in your relationship.

> Don't get stuck in a rut or take each other for granted. Do some of the things you did when you first met: take a leisurely stroll, hand in hand; go to the zoo; play putt-putt; visit a museum; watch a funny movie and laugh together.

> Talk about where you'd like your lives to be in five years, ten years, twenty-five, forty.

> Celebrate every anniversary in a special way. They are milestones in your relationship that you should be proud of and rejoice over.

To My Dear and Loving Husband

If ever two were one, then surely we.
If ever man were loved by wife, then thee;
If ever wife was happy in a man,
Compare with me, ye women, if you can.
I prize thy love more than whole mines of gold
Or all the riches that the East doth hold.
My love is such that rivers cannot quench,
Nor ought but love from thee, give recompense.
Thy love is such I can no way repay,
The heavens reward thee manifold, I pray.
Then while we live, in love let's so persevere
That when we live no more, we may live ever.

ANNE BRADSTREET
American Poet
c. 1612-1672

As the beloved President Abraham Lincoln lay dying from the bullet of John Wilkes Booth, Mary was seen twisting the gold ring on her finger. We can only imagine the thoughts running through her mind at that critical hour. One person in the room declared, "He belongs to the ages," as Lincoln slipped from this life into the next. Mary's thoughts became clear as she countered, "He belongs to me. Our love is eternal."

True Love Lasts Forever

My special friend Don had driven all the way to Las Vegas from Oklahoma to visit me, and after a leisurely dinner at my favorite restaurant, we headed for the desert to park under a brilliant moonlit sky.

"I don't have the right to ask you to marry me," he said. "I have a damaged heart from that time in high school when I had rheumatic fever, and there's a dangerous aneurysm in my throat. The doctor says I could go at any time."

"No, wait …" I said breathlessly. "I give you that right."

"You—you're sure?" His face lit up. "Margaret, will you marry me?"

"Yes!" I answered quickly.

Later Don told me he was so afraid I would never accept his proposal that he told his best friend he was going deer hunting in Nevada. His friend even cleared out a space in his freezer to store the meat.

"I had a successful trip," Don told his buddy when he returned home, "but we won't need the space in your freezer. I went dear hunting, not deer hunting. You spell it d-e-a-r."

Since I had a teaching contract in Las Vegas, it was June before I could move back to Oklahoma and marry Don.

It was a good marriage. We started each day with words of love and tenderness. If we disagreed about something, we talked it over gently and calmly. There were times when Don suffered severe chest pains and I was frightened for him, but the pain would gradually lessen and he would recover.

I especially enjoyed Don's pixie sense of humor. He had a way of making light of his condition that reassured me. One day a small neighbor boy stopped at our gate to talk with Don. He noticed the dangerous bulging vein pulsing in Don's neck.

"Mister," he asked, "what's that thing bobbing up and down in your throat?"

Don regarded the child with a twinkle in his eye. "Oh," he said. "I accidentally swallowed a frog."

During the first year of our marriage, Don opened a television repair shop in Tulsa, and we lived in the small apartment over the shop. Then we decided to buy a small farm, and I took a teaching job in a little country school nearby. Don seemed to thrive on farm life.

We attended a small country church near my school and became fast friends with the young minister. Devoted to his faith, Don was thrilled when the pastor once asked him to speak to the small congregation.

The years slipped by, and gradually my haunting fear for his health diminished. Life was good. We were looking forward to our tenth wedding anniversary one morning in May when Don called out to me before I left for school.

"Wait! I have something for you." He handed me a beautiful bouquet he had picked from our flower garden. "Share these with the kids at school, and remember that I love you."

All day the fragrance of those flowers and the remembrance of those parting words glowed in my heart.

When I returned home that afternoon, I found Don sprawled in his chair as though he were very tired. I thought he was asleep, but when I touched his hand, it was icy cold. I felt for a pulse in his neck, but I knew Don was gone. The dreaded aneurysm had finally burst.

Somehow I lived through those days, weeks, years of grief. But when my life would sink to its lowest ebb, I always felt God's hand at my back, supporting me.

I'm so thankful for the ten years Don and I spent together. Even though he's gone, I know our love is everlasting, just as God promised that He would never leave us nor forsake us.

Since my husband's death I've often thought that if married couples could live each day thinking it might just be their last together, it would make such a difference. Maybe bitter words would be replaced with daily expressions of loving tenderness. It's a good way to live.[18]

He who is filled with love is
filled with God himself.

AUGUSTINE OF HIPPO
Early Writer and Theologian
354-430

We have come to know and have believed the love
which God has for us. God is love, and the one who
abides in love abides in God, and God abides in him.

1 JOHN 4:16 NASB

Love Is God

Love ... trusts God always.

1 CORINTHIANS 13:4,7 THE MESSAGE

*H*eavenly Father,

You describe Yourself in many ways in Your Word, but perhaps the most profound and all-encompassing attribute is that You are love. You don't just have love, You are love! And to think, You live in us!

Show us how we can love each other in the same way that You love us. Cause that love to bear the fruit of patience and kindness; humility and caring; purity and holiness; hope; faithfulness and loyalty; belief in one another; forgiveness; selflessness and service; and wisdom and understanding.

May the love You have for us and the love we share with each other carry us through eternity.
Amen.

Waiting Patiently

I stared at the ivory wedding dress and veil draped over my arm. Instinctively, I knew that I wanted to wear it on my wedding day. Never mind that the idea was ridiculous. Who buys a wedding dress with no prospective groom in sight?

The treasure surfaced during a lunch-hour trip to the resale shop. An innocent search for antique tatting shuttles began a new passion—second-hand store shopping. Soon I started to buy other things including clothing. One day a coworker complimented me on the peach wool suit I was wearing, and I confided that I'd purchased it at a second-hand shop. Impressed, she asked to go with me on my next trip.

That morning had been hectic for both of us—the perfect day to get out of the office during lunch and do a little shopping. Soon we were on our way downtown.

When we arrived, I excused myself and went to the back where the long dresses were hanging. As a vocal soloist, I was building a wardrobe of long dresses and always checked for new additions. That's where I saw it— an ivory wedding dress and veil with an elegant, yet simple, design. The A-line style included one wide panel of lace down the front and matching lace on the short sleeves and around the high neckline. The long veil had matching lace as the headpiece. Enchanted, I knew I wanted to buy it.

Just then, Sandy rounded the corner and stopped to see what I'd found.

"Is that a wedding dress?" she asked.

"Isn't it gorgeous?" I responded, trying to sound casual.

"Go try it on," she said, "I know you want to."

With that encouragement, I slipped into the dressing room and cautiously lowered the dress over my head. It zipped up easily—as if it had been made for me—and I backed against the opposite wall to get a better look in the mirror.

As I opened the curtain and stepped out, Sandy looked me over with wide eyes.

"Oh, Joyce, I know there's no man in your life right now," she said, "but you really must have that dress. You'll be sorry if you don't."

Her comments confirmed what I already knew in my heart. For some reason, God had decided to provide me with a wedding gown for a wedding to someone I had not yet met. I took it for a promise of love and romance yet to come in my life.

That night after modeling both the dress and veil for my mom, I taped two large garbage bags together over them, top and bottom. Then I hung them in the back of my closet, where they could hang freely while I waited for God to send the love of my life across my path.

One, two, then three years passed without incident. Four, five, then six years passed, and I was approaching my thirty-sixth birthday. Still I would pull the dress and veil from the closet and try them on—just to make sure they still fit.

Then one night, a friend asked if I would be interested in a blind date with a man from her office. I wasn't thrilled, having borne many disastrous blind dates in the past. But my date book was all but empty, so I agreed.

Dennis called a few days later, and we made a dinner date for the following Saturday. He arrived—on time—with a charming smile on his face that immediately drew my interest. He seemed perfectly at ease when I introduced him to my mom, and after a few minutes of small talk, we were off.

Dinner was wonderful, but it wasn't the food that I found so appealing; it was the man who had just come walking into my life. After dinner we took a drive and continued our dinner conversation for hours. Three more dates followed the next week—but I knew after the second. This was the man I'd been waiting for. A week later, he proposed.

The next day, I pulled the dress and veil from the back of the closet and took it to the cleaners. I asked the seamstress to take in a few tucks, and add long sleeves, banding them at the wrist with lace. The result was stunning.

On my wedding day, as I stood at the back of the church waiting to go down the aisle, I thought about my impulsive gesture at that thrift shop so many years before. I remembered the many years my beautiful dress and veil had hung in my closet waiting for God to bring by the man I could love forever. I had waited patiently—well, sometimes not so patiently. And yet, here we were. In His perfect timing, God had brought my intended who, at that moment, waited patiently for me to walk down the aisle and take his hand.[19] 💜

For Him and Her

BASED UPON 1 CORINTHIANS 13:4-8 AMP

God is love, and He lives in me. That means that His love lives in me. Because of that, I can love as He loves. Specifically, I can love my sweetheart the way God does.

Because of this, I will endeavor to be compassionate, patient, and kind. I will ask God to help me overcome envy and jealousy and cause my heart to thrill with excitement when the one I love experiences a victory. I pray that God will convict me when I'm behaving in a prideful manner and strip me of arrogance and conceit.

I will strive not to be rude or unmannerly or act in a way that will embarrass the one I love. I won't insist on my own rights or my own way, for I determine to always put my sweetheart first. At the same time, I won't respond by becoming touchy, fretful, or resentful. And I won't keep a mental list of hurts and wrongs.

I determine never to knowingly rejoice at injustice and unrighteousness, but I will take delight when right and truth prevail in our lives together—even when that means exposing my own mistakes and shortcomings.

I will bear up under anything and everything that comes, ever ready to believe the best. My hopes will be fadeless under all circumstances, and I will endure everything without weakening. God's love in me never fades out nor becomes obsolete nor comes to an end.

NOTES

1. Cindy Sigler Dagnan, Oronoga, Missouri. Story used by permission of author.
2. *The Best Loved Poems of the American People* (New York: Doubleday, 1936), p. 43.
3. Susan Duke, Quinlan, Texas. Story used by permission of author.
4. Letter from Robert Browning to Elizabeth Barrett Browning found at http://www.theromantic.com/LoveLetters/browning2.htm (accessed April 20, 2005).
5. Letter from Tsarina Alexandra to Tsar Nicholas II of Russia found at http://www.theromantic.com/LoveLetters/tsarinaalexandra.htm (accessed April 20, 2005).
6. "They Call It Puppy Love" by Rebecca Barlow Jordan was revised and adapted from *Marriage Toners,* published by Fleming H. Revell, 1995, p. 10.
7. *The Best Loved Poems of the American People,* pp. 60-61.
8. Barbara Scott, Springfield, Missouri. Used by permission of the author.
9. Letter from Winston Churchill to his wife found at http://www.theromantic.com/LoveLetters/churchill.htm (accessed April 20, 2005).
10. Letter from Abigail Adams to John Adams, the second president of the United States. Found at http://www.theromantic.com/LoveLetters/adams.htm (accessed April 20, 2005).
11. "When Opposites Attack" by Rebecca Barlow Jordan was revised and adapted from *Courage for the Chicken Hearted* published by Honor Books, 1998, pp. 15-19.
12. Nancy Hoag, Bozeman, Montana. Used by permission of the author.
13. Nancy Hoag, Bozeman, Montana. Used by permission of the author.
14. Jean Wensink, Sheboygan Falls, Wisconsin. Used by permission of the author.
15. Nancy Hoag, Bozeman, Montana. Used by permission of the author.
16. *A Victorian Anthology,* 1837-1895; Edmund Clarence Stedman, ed.; found at http://www.bartleby.com/246/106.html (accessed April 30, 2005).
17. Letter Sullivan Ballou wrote to his wife, Sarah, just one week before he and twenty-seven of his close comrades and 4000 Americans in all would die in the battle at "First Manassas." Found at http://www.theromantic.com/LoveLetters/ballou.htm (accessed April 20, 2005).
18. Margaret Maghe, Okmulgee, Oklahoma. Used by permission of the author.
19. Joyce Ermeling-Heiser, Oconto, Wisconsin. Used by permission of the author.

This and other titles in the Celebration Series
are available from your local bookstore.

Celebrate the Graduate
Celebrate Moms
Celebrate Dads

If this book has touched your life,
we would love to hear from you.
Please send your comments to:
editorialdept@whitestonebooks.com

*"... To him who overcomes I will give some of the hidden manna to
eat. And I will give him a white stone, and on the stone a new name
written which no one knows except him who receives it."*

REVELATION 2:17 NKJV

WHITE STONE BOOKS
LAKELAND, FLORIDA

www.whitestonebooks.com